AUTISM ACTIVITIES WORKBOOK FOR KIDS 8-14

Fun Exercises and Activities for Kids to Build Confidence and Improve Communication Skills

By

Estelle Guzman

TSB PUBLICATIONS

About the Author

A child therapist Dr. Estelle Guzman has learned most of what she knows about life through her longer career. She pursued a master's degree in clinical social work after earning her bachelor's degree. She then went on to get a post-graduate certificate and extra training in applied behavior analysis. Before starting her own private practice, she was able to get valuable experience working in a variety of diverse, inclusive, and demanding settings. In order to improve the lives of the patients she treats, Estelle Guzman continues to stay up-to-date on the most recent research in both her profession and those of associated disciplines. She also uses therapeutic modalities that are evidence-based, moral, culturally sensitive, and socially meaningful. Dr. Estelle Guzman employs humor and a development mentality to keep learning and never give up. With more than ten years of experience in the field of mental health and wellbeing, she also offers support, consultations for parents and caregivers, advocacy, and supervision to other clinicians and interns working in the fields of psychology. In addition, she has been asked to appear as a guest speaker on numerous podcasts as a specialist in mental and behavioral health. In the long run, Estelle Guzman hopes to continue working in the field of mental health and wellbeing as a Licensed Psychotherapist, Behavior Analyst, researcher, writer, and advocate.

CONTENTS

INTRODUCTION

Autistic spectrum disorder (ASD) or Autism is known by difficulties with interpersonal skills, repeated behaviors, language, and nonverbal cues. The Center for Disease Control estimates that 1 in 43 American children currently have autism.

We are aware that there are many different forms of autism, the majority of which are influenced by a combination of inherited and environmental factors. Each autistic person has different skills and challenges because autism is a spectrum disorder. Autism affects how people learn, reason, and solve problems, ranging from severely disabled to well competent. While some people with ASD may require a lot of daily care, others may just require a little assistance and, in some cases, may even be able to live independently.

Various circumstances may cause autism, and it frequently coexists with sensory abnormalities, physical conditions including gastrointestinal (GI) diseases, seizures, or sleep problems, as well as psychological difficulties like anxiety, sadness, and attention deficits.

Autism symptoms typically manifest by the age of two or three. Some related developmental impairments may manifest much sooner and are frequently detectable as young as 18 months. According to research, early intervention helps autistic people achieve their goals later in life.

Youngsters with autism may interact with others differently than typically developing children. Children with autism may not respond to their identities, smile when others smile at them, or pay attention to facial expressions, for instance. They might not employ the motions that developing youngsters usually do, but they frequently find ways of communicating with their parents. To demonstrate something attractive to their parents, for instance, they might lead them by the hand rather than pointing.

Joint attention, which involves making eye contact and movements to share experiences with others, is a skill that autistic children frequently struggle with. Due to these challenges, children with autism may find it more challenging to acquire language and communication skills. For instance, it might be more difficult for a youngster to connect an image of a dog and the word "dog" if the parents point to one aspect of the picture while the child is more interested in another.

Compared to children who are usually developing, many autistic children develop their language abilities more slowly and differently. This implies that they can have trouble understanding what you say to them or obeying your directions. Some autistic children may have trouble using spoken language to request or express their feelings to others.

Children with autism frequently acquire these advanced skills more slowly than children with average development. These variations may impact how well autistic youngsters learn and communicate with adults. For instance, a youngster may be aware that they must summarize a news article for geographical homework but struggle to figure out how to begin; they may have math and English homework but struggle to decide which one to complete first, or they may struggle to cope with mistakes.

Children with autism frequently excel in noticing patterns and small details. For instance, some autistic kids may acquire letters, numbers, and shapes more quickly than typically developing kids. Additionally, some autistic children may pick up on details that normal kids would miss.

Autistic children occasionally can require assistance to see "the larger picture" due to their intense attention to detail. They might take in a lot of information about a situation, but they may not be capable of putting it all together to understand what it all implies. For instance, if kids read story on a butterfly life changes, they can recall that the caterpillar love strawberries but fail to comprehend how the food helps the caterpillar transform into a butterfly.

Not only these conditions but there are many to discuss when it is about development and conditions in autistic children. **Autism Activities Workbook for Kids** will help you to understand your kids' conditions while providing you with the knowledge and worksheets for your kids to overcome their symptoms.

So, continue reading...

Chapter 1: Could My Child Have Autism?

It's critical to seek assistance and support as soon as you can. Early therapy and support are the greatest methods to support and nurture autistic children. That's because they can assist autistic kids in learning the skills necessary for daily life. Children who receive early intervention may occasionally require less or no assistance as they age. Because of neurodiversity, some people process information in their brains differently than others. This causes variations in how people learn, control their emotions, and interact with others. The neurodiversity movement sees autism and other disorders like dyslexia as typical variances in how the brain works.

Ask your family's healthcare nurse or General practitioner about a developmental evaluation if you have concerns about your child's development. The first step in assisting your kid and obtaining services and program appropriate for their needs is obtaining an assessment and diagnosis.

1.1 Autism and Autistic Children

As discussed earlier, a condition that affects a child's nervous system, development, and growth is an autism spectrum disorder (ASD). It frequently manifests in the first three years of a child's life.

Some ASD kids appear to exist in their worlds. They lack social awareness and show no interest in other kids. A child with ASD concentrates on sticking to a schedule, which could involve typical behaviors. A child with an illness frequently struggles with social interaction. They might not speak as early as other kids. They might not want to look people in the eye.

A youngster with ASD may not be able to develop social skills. This is due in part to the possibility that an ASD youngster will struggle to comprehend the emotions or facial expressions of others. A kid with ASD could have:

- Unwillingness to be touched
- A desire to play alone
- Unwillingness to alter routines

Additionally, a youngster with ASD might repeat their actions. This could be done by swaying or flapping one's hands. They might also develop strange attachments to things. But an ASD child might also perform some mental tasks exceptionally well. The kid might, for instance, have stronger counting or measuring skills than other kids. Children with ASD may excel in the arts or music or have an excellent memory for specific information.

Although it can be detected as early as 12 to 18 months, autism is often identified around the age of 2. Multidisciplinary assessments, which are used to examine and evaluate children as part of the diagnosis process, are common. A pediatrician, a psychologist, a speech pathologist, and occasionally a psychiatrist makes up a multidisciplinary team. Other experts, such as an occupational therapist, may also be involved.

These experts may evaluate a youngster concurrently and in the same location. Or they might do individual evaluations over time and in various locations. The experts will share and discuss their findings if the evaluation is conducted this way. A single test does not exist for autism. Rather, a diagnosis is made by;

- Seeing how kids play and interact with one another to understand how kids are growing at the moment.
- Evaluating the history of children's development or how they have grown in the past.
- Speaking with parents.

Children will be given an autistic spectrum disorder diagnosis. Support requirements will be listed along with the diagnosis, ranging from "requiring support" to "requiring very significant support." These levels demonstrate how much support kids require for their restricted, repetitive, or sensory behaviors and their communication and social skills. Health specialists will also evaluate the cognitive and linguistic skills of children.

1.2 Causes and Signs

What specifically causes autism is unknown. Many factors, particularly brain development and genetics, may be to blame.

Early in infancy, particularly in the first three years of life, autistic people's minds develop more quickly than average. This rapid expansion has no apparent cause. However, it suggests that autistic children's brain regions unusually communicate with one another.

There is compelling evidence that autism has a genetic foundation. However, it seems doubtful that a single gene causes autism. It's more likely that numerous genes work in collection to produce an effect. Researchers have identified numerous potential genes as having potential roles in the emergence of autism.

Autism Symptoms

Autism's early warning signs typically develop before a child turns two. Changes in children's communication and social development are among the early warning indicators. Children who eventually receive an autism diagnosis might, for instance:

- Not grin when other people are around
- Make no eye contact
- Not make gestures

Autism symptoms are more obvious in toddlerhood because kids are expected to start talking and interacting with other kids. Children with autism, for instance, might;

- Become unwilling to play with other kids
- Repeat whatever they hear
- Use an odd tone of voice when speaking.

Some kids show many early symptoms, while others show only a few. The symptoms vary depending on the child's age and how autism affects their day-to-day activities.

When youngsters struggle to adjust to novel social settings in the school setting, such as understanding and obeying directions, establishing friends, and having age-appropriate hobbies, older adolescents and children may show signs of autism.

1.3 Diagnosis and Success Story

A single physical exam cannot diagnose ASD. Before age two, healthcare professionals can diagnose ASD in children by following specific standards. The recommendations can aid in an early problem diagnosis. Early ASD diagnosis allows for immediate treatment of affected children.

According to the recommendations, every child should undergo testing for ASD and other developmental abnormalities before the age of two. The examination is conducted during well-child checkups. Children exhibiting developmental or behavioral issues will require additional ASD testing.

Before the age of two, during early check-ups, healthcare professionals look for the following issues:

- By age twelve months, there is no babbling, gesturing, or pointing.
- No words are pronounced at the age of 16 months.
- By 24 months, there are no 2-word sentences, only imitating other people's words or sounds.
- Lack of social or linguistic abilities.
- No eye contact after three to four months.

The healthcare professional will perform additional screening if a youngster exhibits any of the issues above. If your child has ASD or another developmental problem, this will help to demonstrate it. Your child could require the services of a medical professional with specialized knowledge in diagnosing and treating ASD. These screening exams may also be required for your child:

- ❖ Nerve examination
- ❖ Imaging examinations such as MRIs, CT scans, and PET scans.
- ❖ Tests for mental health.
- ❖ Testing for genetic issues that lead to Autism or other behavioral disabilities.

1.4 Tips for the Parents of Autistic Kids

The lifelong nature of ASD can be extremely stressful for the affected individual and their family. The role of primary caregiver for your child will be crucial in helping you and your child. They will aid in your understanding of the process of treatment and childcare services. You are essential to your child's care and well-being. You can assist your child in the following ways:

❖ **Keep team of healthcare practitioners for your child.**

Discuss the additional medical professionals who will be

involved in your child's care with the person who will be caring for your child. A group of professionals may provide care for your kid, including neurosurgeons, speech therapists, vocational and physical therapists, social services, psychiatrists, and psychologists. The care team for your child will be determined by their needs and how severe their ASD is.

Inform people of your child's ASD. Create a therapy plan with the help of your child's doctor, teacher, and other school personnel.

❖ **Look into school resources for your child.**

A child's ASD frequently causes significant interference with their ability to function in typical educational settings. Children with exceptional educational needs may benefit from the Americans with Disabilities Act (ADA) protection. For more information, speak to your child's teacher or school principal.

If your child wanders or struggles to communicate, have them wear a medical alert necklace or bracelet. Consider having them carry a card with contact data and communication symbols in an emergency. Request assistance from the neighborhood community services. ASD may cause stress. It may be beneficial to stay in touch with other parents whose children have ASD.

Take care of yourself and watch for any signs of stress in your loved ones. Giving care can involve a lot of physical and mental labor. Allow loved ones and friends to assist and provide temporary care. It can be beneficial for you and your child to take a break. Obtain more expert assistance as required.

Chapter 2: Autism Effects on a Child's Social Skills

A youngster with ASD has trouble relating to other people. One of the most typical symptoms is difficulty with social skills. They could desire close relationships but are unsure how to go about it.

By the time they are eight to ten months old, your kid may exhibit some social symptoms if they have autism spectrum disorder, such as:

- ❖ When they turn one, they cannot respond to their name.
- ❖ They don't like to be consoled when they are sad.
- ❖ They have no concept of either their own or other people's feelings.
- ❖ Hugs and other forms of physical touch are avoided or rejected.
- ❖ They keep their eyes closed.
- ❖ They are uninterested in playing, sharing, or conversing with others.
- ❖ They favor solitude.
- ❖ They might not extend their arms for assistance with lifting or walking.

2.1 Communication Problems

Between 25 percent and 30 percent of children with autism spectrum disorders start speaking at a young age but later lose those skills, and about 40% of children with autism do not speak at all. Some ASD kids begin talking later in life.

Most people have some communication issues, including:

- ❖ Delayed speech and vocal development.
- ❖ Sing-song, monotone, or computerized speaking voice.
- ❖ Echolalia (reiterating the same sentence over and over).
- ❖ Issues with pronouns, such as speaking "you" instead of "I".
- ❖ Not responding to typical motions (such as pointing or waving) or only doing so occasionally.
- ❖ Inability to remain focused while speaking or responding to inquiries.
- ❖ Not understanding humor or sarcasm.
- ❖ Difficulty communicating wants and emotions.
- ❖ Not understanding cues from expressions, tone of speech, or body language.

2.2 Patterns of Behavior

Additionally, children with ASD exhibit odd behavior or non-typical interests, such as:

- ❖ Repetitive movements such as rocking, jumping, or twirling
- ❖ Pacing constantly and engaging in "hyper" conduct
- ❖ Fixations on particular pursuits or things
- ❖ Certain practices or ceremonies
- ❖ A high threshold for touch, vision, and sound
- ❖ Not engaging in "make-believe" play or acting out other people's behavior
- ❖ Unpredictable feeding patterns
- ❖ Inability to coordinate and clumsiness
- ❖ Impulsiveness (doing without considering)
- ❖ Aggressive actions, both toward oneself and against others
- ❖ Limited ability to focus

2.3 Puberty and Autism

Henry had had a rough start to his academic career. At the age of 9, the boy received an autism diagnosis. He had trouble keeping his emotions in check and processing sensory data in his Tennessee classroom. However, by the time Henry was ten, his parents had discovered strategies for addressing these problems through counseling and medicine.

Then came puberty. Henry developed mood swings and sensitivity. An expressive outburst could be brought on by a perceived snub from a fellow student. He was unable to recover, according to his mother, Elisa. For the remainder of the day, he was upset.

As the young kid grew nearly 6 feet tall, it got harder and harder to control Henry's outbursts. Henry's compulsive behaviors and irritation last year at age fourteen, while he was adjusting to the new medicine, got so bad that Elisa and her husband took him out of school for two weeks. He seemed very depressed, Elisa remembers. "It was terrible." Henry's developing sexuality, which was made more difficult by his difficulties with social skills, added to the chaos. He would deliver a crude joke, not realizing that it might offend his parents. He might propose to a woman he barely knew. Elisa says, "I just hope we can get through this puberty rollercoaster."

For young persons with autism spectrum disorders, puberty can be difficult. It may be challenging to deal with as they sexually grow and become more interested in friendships and dating since they have autism, characterized by sensory and emotional difficulties, repetitive habits, and a lack of social skills. Girls with autism may struggle socially more than other girls because they find it difficult to understand the subtleties of how non-autistic girls communicate. Adolescents with autism are unusually prone to depression, stress, and disordered eating. A 2006 study found that 108 autistic children experienced depression, anxiety, or another mental health disorder in 72 percent of them. Comparatively, a 2017 study of over 50,000 kids and teenagers found that less than 20 percent have a mental health disorder. Teenagers with autism are more likely to experience seizures and cognitive decline.

2.4 Autism Special Needs Checklist

You can anticipate exciting new chances and challenges once your child is prepared for school. The correct educational strategy can enable your child to realize their potential. But studying is not the only purpose of education. Your youngster is negotiating friendships and social settings much like their peers. To assist your child in succeeding during school, adhere to this eight-step checklist.

❖ **Look for assistance from school.**

Many children with autism spectrum disorder get early detection therapy and are diagnosed by age 3. With the aid of a personalized education program, students become qualified for extra services at their neighborhood school system when they are three years old.

Therapy for speech/language, behavior, or sensory issues may be included. Children may receive additional assistance at school from a teaching assistant, a "lunch bunch," or an interpersonal skills group.

Team meets with parents to discuss a child's needs. While you cannot demand specific services, you can challenge the team if you believe it falls short of your child's needs. You can request adjustments before the team is changed each year to ensure your child is on track to accomplish objectives. Not all autistic children require a team.

❖ Addressing Emotional Needs

Your youngster might occasionally feel excluded, behind, or bullied. Children with autism can experience anger or sadness because they sometimes find it difficult to relate to others. If your child exhibits symptoms of depression, such as melancholy, moodiness, or withdrawal, seek help from a qualified counselor. Bullying symptoms include reluctance to attend school, a loss of appetite, difficulty sleeping, and unexplainable sobbing.

Speak with school administration as soon as possible if your child is experiencing bullying or teasing. Use role-playing to explain how to deal with bullies and report issues to teachers, guidance counselors, or other trustworthy people while conversing with your child about the experience at home.

❖ Learn Technology

Children with autism can benefit from technology to become more communicative and social and behave appropriately. Kids may sharpen their focus, get recognized for good conduct, learn new abilities, and have fun by using online educational games, applications, and programs. If a child has difficulty communicating, some gadgets, referred to as "assistive devices," can even vocalize what the child is thinking.

Find out what kinds of applications or other media can benefit your child by speaking with their doctor, speech therapist, or behavioral therapist. The abilities children already learn in school or during treatment sessions are reinforced via several games.

❖ Get Ready for Puberty

Your child will be experiencing new emotions as puberty draws near, which is a typical stage of development. Discuss with your doctor how to handle your child's maturation and what to anticipate. Assure your youngster that puberty brings about typical changes.

When it comes to private actions like getting clothed or contacting private areas, teach your child the distinction between public and personal spaces. Boys might require comfort that wet dreams are acceptable, while girls would need to understand how to change napkins when they start their menstruation.

Discuss with your child what constitutes proper and inappropriate touching and urge them to alert you immediately if somebody steps over the line.

❖ **Get Kids Moving**

Children with autism benefit greatly from physical activity since it can increase their strength, dexterity, endurance, and body awareness. Obesity in children can be prevented with regular exercise. Additionally, exercise may increase focus and reduce repetitive, self-stimulating activities.

Numerous sports organizations can encourage your child to be fit and healthy while making new friends who face comparable difficulties. Kids can stay active by participating in karate, rehabilitative horse riding, and water therapy.

❖ **Schedule social events and playdates**

Even though it can occasionally be difficult, children with autism must interact with their peers. Playdates and other events provide much-needed opportunities for social skill development and friend-making. Those with trouble can join a social skills group, which offers assistance with making introductions, conversing with others, recognizing social cues, and more.

When choosing a playmate for your child, search for someone with similar interests. Pre-plan the activities (such as taking your child to a park, playground, or another area they will enjoy) and stay away from places with a lot of noise and excitement if you believe it would overwhelm them. Give your child a heads-up on what to anticipate. If you want to "inform ahead" of time what will happen during a playdate, think about creating a visual plan with photos or making social stories.

❖ **Seek Support.**

Parenting a child with autism can be difficult daily. Even on the hardest days, a solid support system may help you get through it. Find a local support network or join a local, national autism awareness organization branch to connect with other families who can relate to your situation. If there isn't a local support network, look on the internet.

❖ **Ensure the Future of Your Child**

It's not too late to create a will or a financial and legal structure for your child's future. To determine the best method to handle your assets and make financial preparations for your child's future, consult a financial advisor and lawyer specializing in special needs legislation.

Chapter 3: The Link: Autism and Anxiety

Anxiety can affect anyone. Anxiety is a frequent feeling when confronted with a demanding or stressful environment. However, some autistic people may experience anxiety daily due to adjusting to potentially demanding social and sensory surroundings. According to studies, autistic people are more likely to feel anxiety, and approximately half of all autistic people are thought to experience significant worry regularly.

3.1 Understanding and Managing Anxiety

40 percent of young people with ASD exhibit clinically increased levels of anxiety or at least one chronic anxiety, particularly obsessive-compulsive disorder, even though anxiety is not considered a key characteristic of ASD. Since anxiety significantly influences the course and core characteristics of the disorder, aggravating psychosocial problems and repetitive behaviors, it is especially crucial to identify and treat anxiety in ASD.

Additionally, while uncontrolled comorbid anxiety has been linked to the emergence of despair, aggressiveness, and self-harm in ASD, early identification and therapy may offer these individuals a better prognosis.

❖ **How Anxiety Develops in ASD and How to Spot It**

Due to overlapping symptomatology and different symptom presentations in patients with ASD, it can be challenging to identify the presence of anxiety. Patients with limited verbal skills may be unable to communicate their internal feelings, such as fear, and instead, exhibit their uneasiness through disruptive behaviors. Conversely, some verbally proficient patients may struggle to comprehend and articulate their emotions.

Typically, anxiety may manifest differently at various points along the course of ASD and in connection with various environmental demands:

Phobias may trigger ASD due to excessive sensitivity to sensory stimuli, such as a loud environment. Specific phobias in these patients typically involve extremely unusual stimuli (such as commercial jingles, balloons bursting, vacuum cleaners, flushing toilets, alarm systems at school, etc.), but they may also present fears (such as of the dark, invertebrates)

Obsessive-compulsive disorder (OCD), characterized by intrusive and unwelcome thoughts and ensuing compulsive behaviors, frequently coexists with autism spectrum disorder (ASD). It is crucial to recognize comorbid OCD in these patients because, unlike repetitive behaviors typical of ASD, compulsions are used as a coping mechanism to reduce anxiety.

Social anxiety: As the patient matures and the environment demands more of them, social communication deficit may highlight the emergence of social anxiety, particularly if the patient is truly powerful and conscious of their social inadequacy. In addition to limiting the patient's opportunity to practice interpersonal skills, social phobia, defined as strenuous anxiety or fear of being adversely affected in a social or performance situation, also makes people avoid social situations, which increases the risk of negative peer responses and even bullying.

Separation anxiety can develop when a person must separate from emotional support, such as when leaving home for school. Social impairment may cause overprotective responses from parents, reinforcing the child's avoidance behavior.

Other atypical anxiety symptoms include severe levels of distress caused by changes in a person's routine or environment, which children and young adults with ASD frequently experience.

❖ **How to recognize anxiety triggers?**

One of the first steps in lowering your child's stress and helping them handle it is figuring out what makes your autistic child uneasy. You may need to interpret your child's signs and figure out what makes them anxious or tense because autistic kids and teenagers sometimes struggle to understand and control their emotions.

Children with autism who frequently experience anxiety include:

- ❖ Routine adjustments, such as skipping a weekly piano session because the instructor is unwell.
- ❖ Changes to the environment, such as a new home, new playground equipment at the neighborhood park, or furniture rearranged at home.
- ❖ Unfamiliar social situations, such as a birthday celebration at a stranger's home.
- ❖ Sensory sensitivity, such as an aversion to certain sounds, bright lights, smells, or food textures.
- ❖ Fear of a certain circumstance, behavior, or thing, such as sleeping in their bed, using the restroom, balloons, or vacuum cleaners.
- ❖ Moments of change include the start of a new academic year, the start of secondary school, or the onset of puberty.

Making a list of the circumstances that make your child uneasy can be helpful once you've identified some of them so that you can figure out how to help your child cope with them. Give your youngster many chances to practice handling these items and circumstances in secure settings.

It is beneficial if the other caregivers for your child, such as teachers, daycare providers, and family members, are also aware of the triggers for their anxiety and what they can do to support them in doing so.

3.2 Activities and Exercises to Overcome Anxiety

Anxiety Worksheet

Think of a situation that made you anxious and answer the questions.

Anxiety Worksheet

What Happened

_____

_____

_____

How I Reacted

_____

_____

_____

How Bad is it Really?	What I Think/Feel	How I'd Like to React Next Time
Not Bad	_____	_____
①	_____	_____
②	_____	_____
③	_____	_____
④	_____	_____
⑤	_____	_____
Really Bad	_____	_____

Anxiety Buster

WORKSHEET

TOP STRESSES

WHAT CAN BE DONE?

_____   _____

_____   _____

_____   _____

_____   _____

TO DO: Write everything swirling in your mind. Seeing it on paper helps things seem more manageable.

_____   _____

_____   _____

_____   _____

_____   _____

_____   _____

TOP 3 PRIORITIES TODAY: Instead of trying to do it all, pick 3. Accomplishment increases dopamine!

01. _____   02. _____   03. _____

Anxiety Breakdown

What is making me feel anxious?

_____

What are some of the negative thoughts that I am having?

How is my body responding?

_____

_____

What is the worst thing that can happen?

_____

What do I have in my control to keep this from happening?

_____

_____

What are positive thoughts to help calm my mind?

_____

What are positive thoughts to help calm my mind?

_____

30 Days to Worry

Use this monthly worksheet to keep track of your worries. Each day that you worry about something, write it down. Each day that you don't worry, skip it and leave it blank.

How do you feel about your thought patterns this past month?

_____

_____

I Can Cope! with feeling ANXIOUS

Some things that make me feel anxious are......

1. _____

2. _____

3. _____

These changes happen when I feel anxious:

Changes in my body...	Thoughts I have...	Things I do...

When I feel anxious, I can cope by:

Check all of the coping skills that might be helpful! Use the blank spaces to write in your own

☐ Deep breathing   ☐ Going to walk   _____

☐ Using positive self-talk ☐ Writing in my journal   _____

☐ Meditating or relaxing   ☐ Practicing mindfulness _____

☐ Talking to a friend   ☐ Thinking happy thoughts _____

☐ Talking to an adult   ☐ Keeping myself busy   _____

☐ Playing a game   ☐ Exercising   _____

JUST BECAUSE...

What assumptions do people make about you when they see you?

What type of person do they think you are because of your skin color, gender, speech, facial features, weight, etc.?

Just because I'm ⬭⬭⬭⬭⬭ ,people think that I

⬭⬭⬭⬭⬭⬭⬭⬭⬭⬭⬭⬭⬭⬭⬭⬭⬭⬭⬭⬭

,but the truth is ⬭⬭⬭⬭⬭⬭⬭⬭⬭

Just because I'm ⬭⬭⬭⬭⬭ ,people think that I

⬭⬭⬭⬭⬭⬭⬭⬭⬭⬭⬭⬭⬭⬭⬭⬭⬭⬭⬭⬭

,but the truth is ⬭⬭⬭⬭⬭⬭⬭⬭⬭

Just because I'm ⬭⬭⬭⬭⬭ ,people think that I

⬭⬭⬭⬭⬭⬭⬭⬭⬭⬭⬭⬭⬭⬭⬭⬭⬭⬭⬭⬭

,but the truth is ⬭⬭⬭⬭⬭⬭⬭⬭⬭

How can you respond whenever people make these assumptions about you?

More & Less

Use this worksheet to explore changes that you would like to make as you work towards the type of person that you'd like to be. What are behaviors or traits that you wish you had or could increase? What things do you wish you would do less? Talk about what would happen if you made these changes.

I wish I was more...

1. _____because _____

2. _____because _____

3. _____because _____

4. _____because _____

5. _____because _____

I wish I was less...

1. _____because _____

2. _____because _____

3. _____because _____

4. _____because _____

5. _____because _____

If I made these changes_____

_____

I Feel... When

I feel happy when_____

I feel angry when_____

I feel super excited when _____

I feel sad when _____

I feel surprised when_____

I feel scared when_____

3.3 Coping Strategies for Anxiety

When your child starts to feel worried or agitated, you can help them learn how to relax. These could consist of the following:

- ❖ Five trips around the yard running.
- ❖ Performing 50 trampoline jumps.
- ❖ Slowly counting up to ten.
- ❖ Five full breaths.
- ❖ Examining a collection of special or preferred items.
- ❖ Reading favorite book.
- ❖ Closing eyes for short time.
- ❖ Visiting a peaceful area of the house.

Encourage your child to use these techniques while they're calm. You can gently encourage your child to use the tactics when they feel nervous after they are fully acquainted with them.

Chapter 4: The Connection: Autism and Depression

Autistic people are four times more likely to develop depression in their lifetime as compared to their neurotypical colleagues. However, nothing is known about why or the best ways to assist. Autism spectrum illness and depression can coexist. It poses certain particular difficulties for patients, professionals, and caretakers. People who also exhibit autism traits may find it more challenging to identify the symptoms and signs of depression. There is limited study on how autism and depression may alter treatment outcomes, even though depressive disorders are treated similarly in people with and without autism.

4.1 Understanding and Managing Depression

One of the most prevalent psychiatric diseases in the United States is depression. In the past year, at least one severe depressive episode was experienced by about 7 percent of all American adults. Autism patients have a higher incidence of depression.

According to psychologists, who presented a webinar on anxiety, depression, and sleep, people with autism may experience depressive episodes three times more frequently than people in the general community.

Why is the problem existing?

Numerous theories exist. Many autistic persons, according to psychologists are excellent at paying attention to detail and concentrating on a subject or idea. While this can be a useful talent, it also increases the likelihood of depression in those with autism. Rumination, or repeatedly thinking about a bad experience or emotion, plays a significant role in depression. People with autism may be more likely to feel depressed if they become concentrate on unpleasant memories. Some individuals with autism might also have executive function issues, making it challenging to divert their attention away from rumination.

Self-reported social deficits predicted sadness in people with autism spectrum disorder when symptom intensity and cognitive capacity were considered, according to a study of adults with autism. These results imply that increased self-perceived social deficits in ASD are associated with depressive illnesses. For some people with autism, the need to interact in specific ways may make social relationships more challenging. Feelings of loneliness, exclusion, or isolation may result from a lack of resources and assistance for ASD-related issues, resulting in depression.

❖ How Can Depression Be Recognized?

Depression symptoms might be easy to recognize or difficult to identify. Some people with autism, especially young children, may find it difficult to understand or express their emotions. Individuals and caregivers can watch for behavioral changes that could be signs of depression. Changes in hunger, weight, sleep, energy or interest are just a few examples.

Sometimes, signs of depression include fatigue or agitation. Pay attention to how these actions alter over time and whether a clear cause can be found. For instance, staying up late to study for exams may result in fatigue and a rise in appetite. The symptoms in that situation have a known etiology. If they last for several weeks, they might be symptoms of depression or another mental illness.

To keep track of your emotions and actions, think about journaling. Changes in sleep habits, hunger, weight, interest, and general mood should be noted in written records as they are typically more trustworthy than recollection or casual observation.

❖ Autism, Depression, and a Higher Risk of Suicide

The likelihood of suicidal tendencies must be addressed while considering the diagnosis and treatment of depression. Psychiatrists are taught in medical school to determine the risk of suicide in each patient we examine for depression. This also holds for the evaluation of people with ASD.

Several risk factors for suicidal thoughts and attempts in kids with ASD were identified by psychologists in a recent study that was published in the journal Research in Autism Spectrum Disorders. The researchers interviewed parents of 791 autistic children, 186 generally developing children, and 35 non-autistic children diagnosed with depression.

The percentage of kids trying to take their own lives was 28 times higher for kids with autism as compared to kids with usual development. Compared to youngsters who weren't autistic but had depression, it was three times lower in those with autism. Among autistic youngsters, depression was also the most powerful predictor of suicidal ideas or actions. Luckily, children under the age of 10 rarely displayed suicidal impulses.

These findings highlight the significance of doctors considering the risk of suicide when assessing adolescents or adults with ASD. Yes, it is difficult to accurately diagnose the depression and suicide risks that are present in ASD patients.

Depressive Symptoms Worksheet

Depressive symptoms can be grouped into 3 possible categories. Some symptoms are of the physiological type, which are those that have something to do with physical sensations or your physical body, for example: Insomnia, poor appetite, or low energy level. Some symptoms are of the cognitive (thoughts) and affective (emotions) type, such as: thoughts of sudden, haplessness, feeling sad and crying. The third category of symptoms is related to how you act and behave, for example: staying in bed, not going out, avoiding people.

What do YOU experience, when you are depressed?

Physiological	Cognitive/ Affective	Behavioral
_____	_____	_____
_____	_____	_____
_____	_____	_____
_____	_____	_____
_____	_____	_____
_____	_____	_____
_____	_____	_____
_____	_____	_____
_____	_____	_____
_____	_____	_____

Depressive Thoughts Breakdown

Depression Vs. Truth

Depression often lies to us. Depression can make us feel like we are worthless, or that our situation is permanent and we will never feel better. Write down some of your depressive thoughts. Then write down some alternative thoughts that are more balanced and truthful about your situation.

Automatic Negative Thoughts

Automatic negative thoughts (ANTS) are thoughts that pop in our head without effort, that make us feel down or depressed. Use questions to challenge these unhelpful thoughts to come up with something more positive and encouraging!

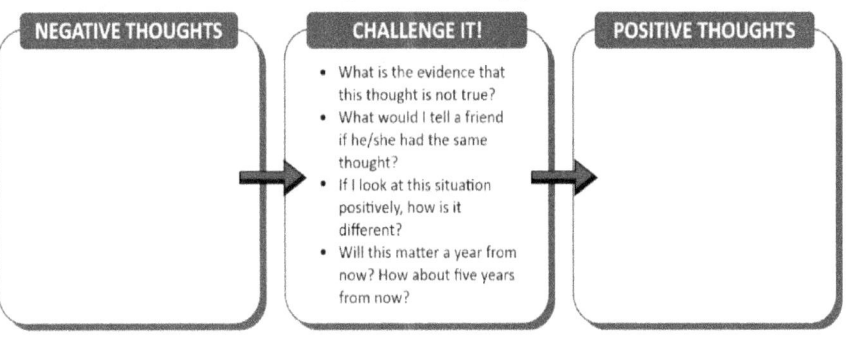

NEGATIVE THOUGHTS

CHALLENGE IT!
- What is the evidence that this thought is not true?
- What would I tell a friend if he/she had the same thought?
- If I look at this situation positively, how is it different?
- Will this matter a year from now? How about five years from now?

POSITIVE THOUGHTS

Encouraging Thoughts

When you feel down or depressed, negative thoughts often flow through your mind. What are some encouraging thoughts you can have to help you feel better when you are depressed?

Challenging Negative Thoughts

Change your thoughts, change your reality.

What am I upset/worried about?

_____

_____

_____

How are my emotions affecting my behavior?

_____

_____

_____

How are my beliefs/expectations irrational in this situation?

_____

_____

_____

What is a more positive, realistic way of viewing this situation?

_____

_____

_____

I Am Someone Who...

Complete the sentences below to share more about yourself

I am someone who loves_____

I am someone who hates_____

I am someone who can't_____

I am someone who can_____

I am someone who will never_____

I am someone who has_____

I am someone who cant 't wait to _____

I am someone I am someone who would rather_____ than_____

I am someone who has never_____

I am someone who wishes_____

I am someone who tried to_____

I am someone whom nobody seems to _____

I am someone whom everybody seems to_____

I am someone who just can't get enough_____

I am someone who doesn't know how to_____

I am someone who usually forgets to_____

I am someone who never forgets to_____

I am someone who is thankful for_____

I am someone who will probably end up_____

I am_____

Teenage Depression

I'm stressed out!
Help me!

1. Can you suggest three reasons why many teenagers feel stressed?

- ———————————————————
- ———————————————————
- ———————————————————

2. Put a tick (✓) next to the way you think it works. Why do they work?

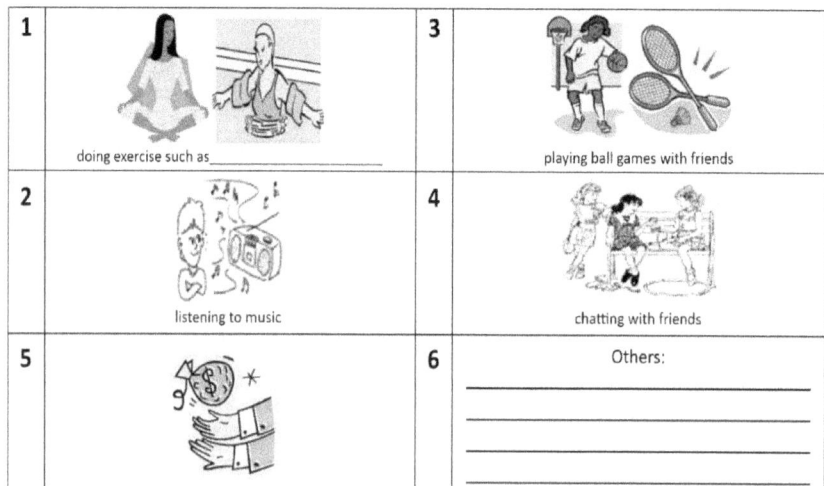

Why do the methods you ticked work?

————————————————————————————————

————————————————————————————————

44

Behavioral Activation

You can begin to decrease depression by engaging in activities you find enjoyable, and by taking care of responsibilities that you have been neglecting

List three activities you enjoy:

1.

2.

3.

List three responsibilities you need to take care of:

1.

2.

3.

Try doing at least one activity or responsibility each day. Use the following scale to rate your depression, pleasant feelings, and sense of achievement before and after the activity.

0	1	2	3	4	5	6	7	8
None	Minimal	Slight	Mild	Moderate	A Lot	Higher	Very High	Extreme

Activity (location, date, time)		Depression	Pleasure	Achievement
	Before			
	After			
	Before			
	After			
	Before			
	After			

Depression Worksheet
Challenging Depressing Thoughts

Objectives: To help an individual challenge his depressing thoughts to eliminate their effects on him.

Instruction: In the table given below, mention the depressing thoughts that come across your mind frequently. Challenge these thoughts with more positive and rational thoughts.

Depressing Thoughts	Challenging Thoughts

I FEEL SAD TODAY!

Answer these questions to help you explore your feelings of sadness today.

What happened to make you feel sad?

_____

_____

_____

What other feelings are you experiencing?

_____   _____   _____

How long have you been feeling this way?_____

What has happened to make it better?_____

_____

What has happened to make it worse?_____

_____

What do you need right now?_____

_____

What can you do to start feeling better?

(1) _____   (2) _____

(3) _____   (4) _____

Jumping to Conclusions:

When you tell yourself you can predict the future or the outcome of an event.

How to Change it

☐ Consider the odds of your predication coming true.

☐ Look at the evidence against your negative thought.

Write your negative thought and then dispute it.

Even though I think _____

_____

The truth is _____

_____

_____

_____

FEELING OF THE DAY: "SAD"

Sad means: **feeling unhappy, feeling upset about something.**

What does feeling sad mean to me?

When do I feel sad?

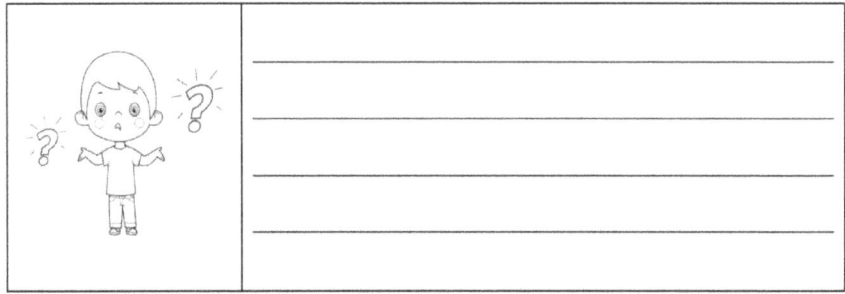

Preparing For
Sad Or Negative Feelings

It can sometimes be helpful to create a plan for times when you are feeling down. Answer the questions below to come up with a plan to improve your mood and cope with difficult situations.

What situations or triggers might make me feel sad or depressed?

What do I usually do when faced with sad or negative feelings?

What are some positive things I can do when I am feeling sad or down?

Who are some people I can contact for support, and how do I get in contact with them?

What should I avoid when feeling sad or down?

What can I say to encourage myself to stay calm?

Coping skills I can use if I start to feel sad or depressed:

Relaxation Skills	Positive Enjoyable Activities	Good Health Habits	Thinking Skills
1._____	1._____	1._____	1._____
2._____	2._____	2._____	2._____

Other: 1._____   2._____   3._____

4.3 Coping Strategies for Depression

Autism-related depression is treated with methods comparable to the general depression. A minor alteration may be required to account for variations in thinking, communicating, or behaving.

It has been demonstrated that _psychotherapy_, more specifically altered cognitive behavioral therapy, is useful in treating depression in people with an autism spectrum disorder.

CBT and other psychotherapies can address rumination and other depression-related cognitive processes.

Medication. When taken in conjunction with therapy, antidepressant medications are most effective. Research shows that using medications alone may not be as helpful as other treatments. The potential and negative effects of medication for depression in autistic people require further study.

A mix of _Medication and Psychotherapy_ - Studies have indicated that one of the more successful therapies for depression is a mixture of psychotherapy and medication.

Chapter 5: Autism and Attention Issues

The prevalence of ADHD symptoms among those with an ASD diagnosis is greater than 50%. ADHD is the comorbidity disorder that affects children with ASD most frequently. However, up to 25% of children with ADHD also show low-level ASD signs, such as social difficulties or an increased sensitivity to clothing textures.

5.1 Co-Occurrence and Management of ADHD and Autism

Both Autism and ADHD are neurodevelopmental disorders. Both diseases/disorders consequently have an effect on the central nervous system, which controls activities including language, recollection, human engagement, and focus. Numerous scientific studies have shown that the two illnesses frequently coexist even if their underlying causes are still unclear.

Autism or ADHD have affected brain development in some way. That includes executive functioning, which is crucial because it controls impulsive behavior, decision-making, time management, focus, and organizing skills. Social skills are impacted by many children. Autism and ADHD are more prevalent among boys.

Although adults may experience ADHD or ASD, this is less common than in children. While ASD is a lifetime illness, extensive study has shown that one of children with ADHD continue to experience symptoms into adulthood.

❖ **What Distinctions Exist Between ASD and ADHD?**

Because their conduct differs from that of their classmates, many kids receive their initial diagnosis of ADHD around the time they begin preschool or kindergarten. Children with ADHD may exhibit constant agitation, impulsivity, and attention struggles. However, some kids with ADHD exhibit various symptoms, such as concentrating all their attention on a single object and refusing to play with other toys.

Before they turn two years old, some children with ASD start to show symptoms. Others may not exhibit symptoms of ASD until they are old enough to attend school and their social behaviors stand out from those of their peers. Children with ASD frequently avoid eye contact and don't seem motivated to interact with others or play. It's possible for their speech to develop slowly or not at all. They could be concerned with repetitive movements, particularly with their fingers and hands, or the similarity of food textures.

❖ Knowing The Combination

Medical professionals were hesitant to label a child as having both ADHD and ASD for a long time. Because of this, very few medical researchers have examined how comorbid disorders affect children and adults. For many years, the American Psychiatric Association (APA) insisted that the two disorders couldn't coexist in the same person. The APA revised its position in 2013. The Diagnostic and Statistical Manual of Mental Disorders (DSM-5) was recently released, and the APA claims that the two disorders can co-occur.

In a review of studies published in 2015, researchers have found that between forty and Fifty percent of individuals with ASD also exhibit symptoms of ADHD. Neither the source of each ailment nor the reason why they co-occur so frequently is fully understood by researchers. Genetics may play a role in both illnesses. An uncommon gene that may be connected to both diseases was discovered in one study. This discovery might help to understand why certain illnesses frequently affect the same person. More study is still required for a better understanding of the relationship between ADHD and ASD.

❖ **ADHD- and ASD-Specific Behaviors**

Children with ADHD frequently struggle to focus on a single activity or task. They could be easily distracted when going about their everyday business. Children with ADHD find it difficult to finish one task before moving on to another and frequently find it difficult to stay still for long periods. However, some kids with ADHD could be so engrossed in a subject or activity that they hyper-focus on it or obsess about it. Although concentrating on one item can be beneficial, it could mean that kids find it challenging to switch their focus to other tasks when asked to.

Most likely, children with autism will be overly focused and unable to change their focus to the next task. They frequently have a low tolerance for change and are rigid about their habits. It can entail eating the same meals and traveling the same route each day. Many have a strong sensitivity to or insensitivity to light, sound, contact, discomfort, smell, or taste. They might have predetermined food tastes based on color or texture and use gestures like repetitive hand flapping. Due to their strong focus, individuals with ASD frequently have long-term memory for specific information and may excel in math, science, art, and music.

5.2 Activities and Exercises to Overcome Attention Issues

Below are some attention and focus related exercises for kids to handle ADHD with Autism.

Arrows

Draw the shapes by looking at the arrow directions.

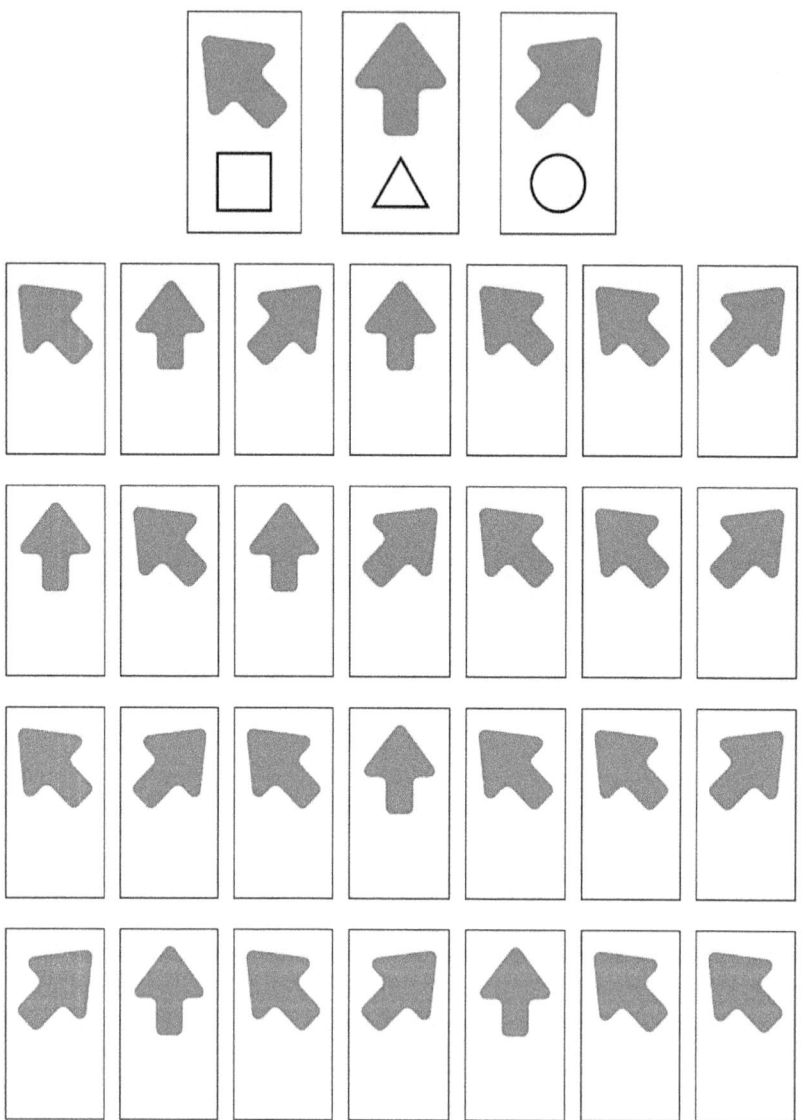

Rehabilitation Worksheet

⑮

⑭　　　　　　　　　⑯　　①

　　　㉓　　　⑦

⑬

　　　　　　　　⑥

㉔

⑫　　　⑧

　　　　②　　　　㉒

㉕　　③

　　　⑰　　　⑤

⑨

　　　　⑱

⑩

⑪　　　⑲　　　④　　㉑

　　⑳

57

Air Balloon Worksheet

Write the math signs by examining the balloon colors.

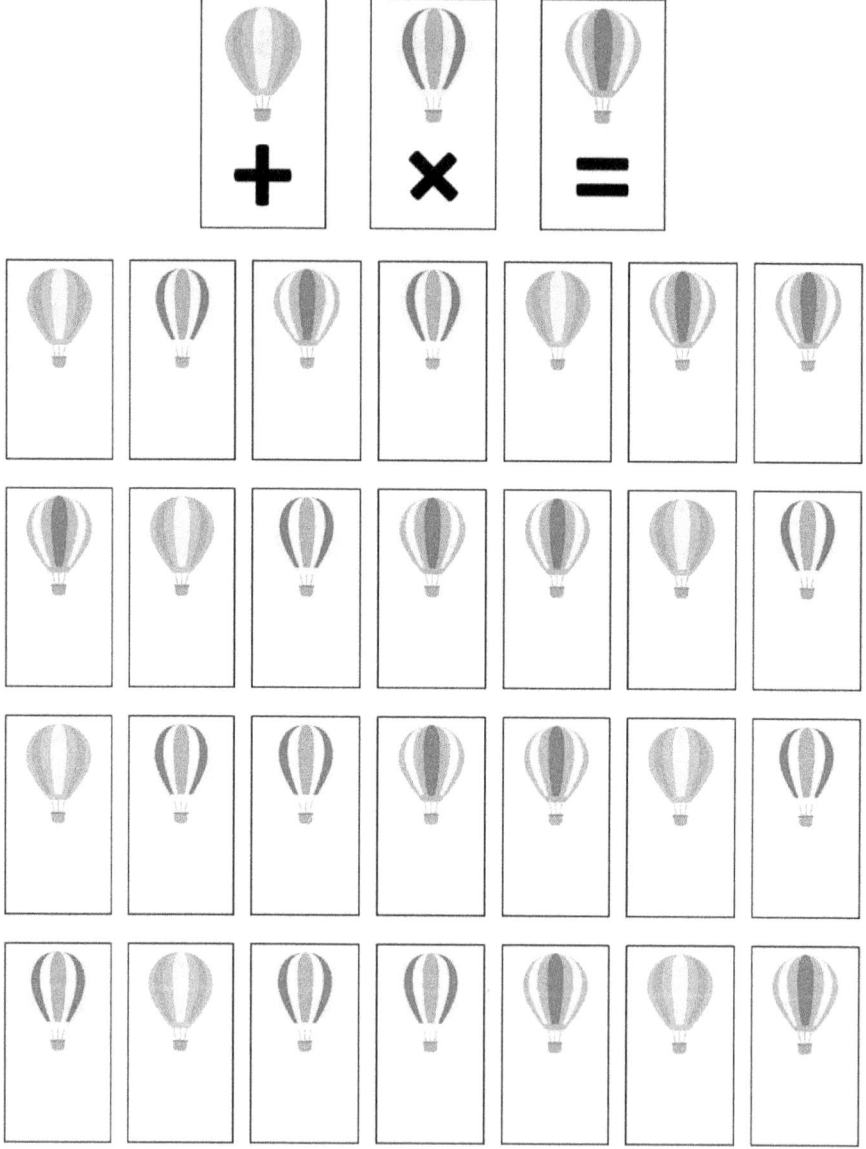

Copy the given pattern.

Follow the path

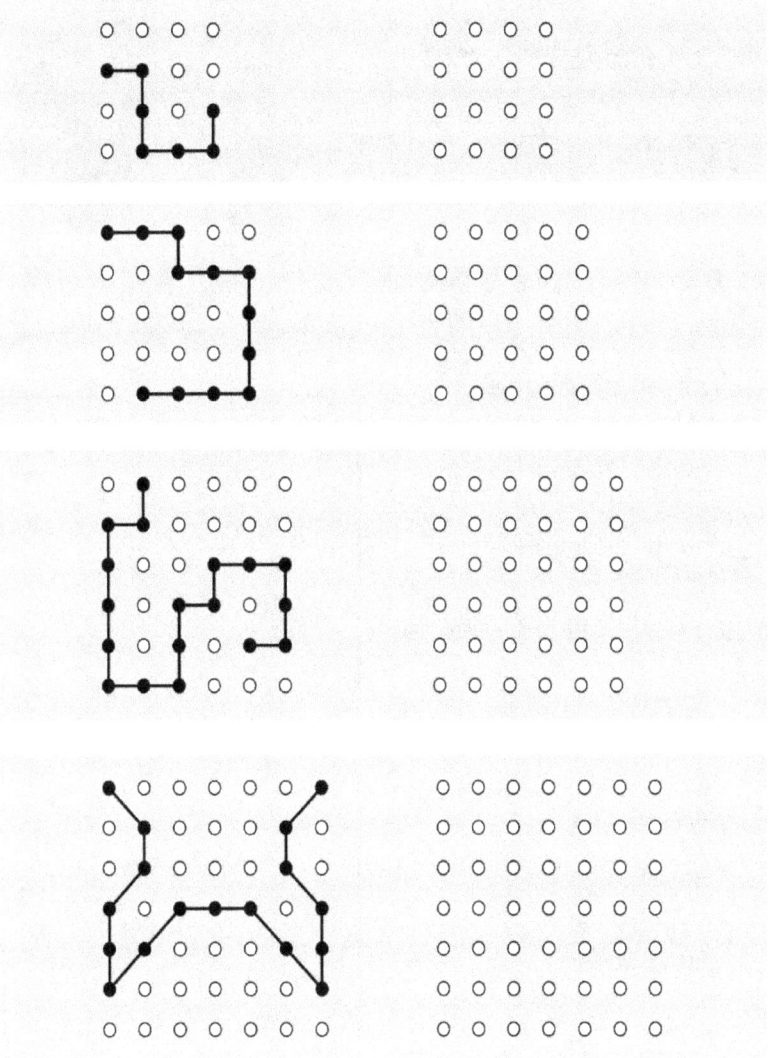

Attention: Rating Scale

Attention is the ability to pay attention and focus without being distracted for reasonable amounts of time.

1) Rate yourself on each of the attention skills listed.

2) Circle the ones you feel you could improve upon.

Write a goal about how you could improve your attention and focus skills, be specific and indicate the strategies you could use in the box to the right.

❶ Agree ❷ Somewhat Agree ❸ Disagree

_____ I am not easily distracted

_____ I focus on the task at hand

_____ I have strategies to deal with distractions

_____ I can concentrate to complete tasks

_____ I am mindful and stay present without daydreaming or losing focus

_____ I am able to tune out unnecessary details or noises

_____ I can concentrate easily

_____ I rarely daydream

_____ _____
              Other

60

5.3 Coping Strategies for ADHD

You must take care of yourself to perform at your peak when tackling unpredictable situations. Each person's version of effective self-care is different, but it all aims to preserve good mental, emotional, and physical health. It could appear as follows:

❖ Taking little rest periods during the day.

❖ Breathing techniques training. Examples: Slowly breathe deeply. Inhale peace as you breathe, and exhale tension. Three times, please. Take a breath in and clench your fists. Release your fists and take a deep breath. Three times, repeat.

❖ Taking part in physical activity

❖ Journaling

❖ Maintaining a specified goal planner

❖ If necessary, use organizers.

❖ Keep in touch with the people who are essential to you, such as your family, friends, and supporters.

❖ Take care not to merge with or take on other people's angst. The idea that autistic persons are unable to understand the feelings of others is untrue. Many individuals with autism mistakenly assume that the situation is exactly the opposite: we may feel intense fusing and take in other people's feelings a little too much, which causes overwhelm and shutdown.

❖ Create a comparison between plans A and B. Your "A" plan for life has essentially been destroyed due to health issues. Now is the time to plan and think about your life (plan B).

❖ On bright, sunny days, go outside (in a safe manner). Nature has the power to heal. Bring gloves and masks anytime you go outside, whether walking or riding a bike, and keep a safe physical distance.

❖ Acknowledge that maintaining safety involves extra mental effort. My friend and colleague says that the autistic mind is like a "cognitive rain bucket." For instance, there is a lot more planning required now rather than simply heading to the shop like we used to. To stay safe, we must consider using masks, avoiding close contact with others, and many other factors. Ultimately, we have used up all our energy and might not have much left to do other things. Reducing our expectations is related to realizing that more effort is needed.

❖ Many adults with autism are turning more frequently to calming and coping mechanisms. Although some people might think they are "regressing" back to these behaviors, this is untrue. In these stressful moments, autistic people need to permit themselves to engage in self-regulatory activities; therefore, feel free to self-stim! When leaving, keep things simple. Bring as little as you can when heading out, except essentials.

Chapter 6: Emotional Ties: Autism and Other Mental Issues

Autism is a component of or closely linked to at least seven other illnesses. Each disease has its distinct symptoms, as well as those that are frequently associated with autism. Autism spectrum disorder is frequently accompanied by medical comorbidities, such as ADD/ADHD, seizures, dental problems, sleep disorders, and gastrointestinal complaints. The following conditions all share behavioral traits with an autism spectrum disorder. These illnesses' behavioral therapies overlap with autism. However, the diagnosis should always guide treatment. Before beginning any course of treatment, it is crucial to acquire a diagnosis from a licensed healthcare expert.

❖ Bipolar Disorder and Autism

Mania — a frantic state known as bipolar disorder — and depressive episodes frequently occur back-to-back in those with the illness.

Examining the onset and duration of the symptoms makes it crucial to distinguish between those of real bipolar disorder and those of autism. For instance, a child with autism may exhibit constant high energy and invasive social behavior throughout childhood. As a result, rather than being a sign of a manic mood fluctuation, her propensity to chat with strangers and make offensive comments is probably a feature of her autism.

Treatments: For some people with autism who have trouble understanding and expressing feelings, several drugs used to treat bipolar illness can be troublesome. Additionally, perhaps safer drugs can be given by a psychiatrist.

❖ Schizophrenia and Autism

Both autism and schizophrenia have difficulties interpreting language and comprehending the emotions and thoughts of others. The psychosis associated with schizophrenia frequently incorporates hallucinations, which is an obvious distinction. Additionally, schizophrenia first manifests in early adulthood, whereas the fundamental symptoms of autism often appear between 1 and 3 years of age.

❖ Disorder of Compulsive Behavior (OCD)

According to research, adults and teenagers with autism are more likely than the general population to have OCD. However, it can be challenging to tell the difference between OCD symptoms and the repetitive actions and constrained interests that characterize autism.

We strongly advise that you seek evaluation from a mental health professional with expertise in autism and OCD if you believe that you or your kid has developed OCD in conjunction with autism.

❖ Epilepsy and Seizures

The term "epilepsy" refers to various brain diseases when a kid experiences, or is at risk of experiencing, frequent, erratic seizures due to aberrant electrical activity in the brain.

Aberrant electrical activity in the brain brings strange sensations and atypical movement or behavior. These are referred to as seizures or convulsions. A youngster typically experiences a brief period of consciousness, a body convulsion, odd motions, or bouts of gazing during seizures.

Because some seizure symptoms resemble autism symptoms, such as failing to answer your name or engaging in repetitive, tic-like activities, it can be challenging to diagnose epilepsy in autistic children.

But,

How prevalent are seizures and epilepsy in kids with autism?

20–30% of those with autism have seizures. Children under five years old and teenagers experience seizures the most frequently. Epilepsy is more likely to occur in autistic people with mild to severe intellectual handicaps, neurological disorders (such as cerebral palsy), or children who regress in their skills. Additionally, there may be a genetic link between seizures and autism.

Anti-epileptic medication is frequently used in treatment. You can take certain actions to lessen the consequences of epilepsy. Making sure your child takes their medications on time, gets an adequate amount of rest, and stays away from stressful circumstances are a few of them.

6.1 Autism and Other Health Conditions

❖ **Syndrome Prader-Willi**

While not a subtype of autism, Prader-Willi syndrome is a condition that occasionally coexists with it. This disorder's typical symptoms include a compact body type, undeveloped sexual traits, weak muscular tone, and an obsession with food that is frequently accompanied by impulsive eating. Many Prader-Willi Syndrome patients are overweight due to their fascination with eating. Mild mental deficiencies are common in Prader-Willi Syndrome patients.

The following behaviors are some of those shared by both Prader-Willi syndrome and autism:

- Verbal and motor development lags.
- Schooling difficulties, infant feeding issues, sleep issues, skin plucking, and tantrums.
- Strong tolerance for pain.

The prevalence of Prader-Willi syndrome is one in 10,000. A little chunk of chromosome 15 that appears to come from the paternal side of the family is absent in most people with this condition. The person may have Angelman Syndrome if missing a tiny chunk of chromosome 15 on the maternal side.

Behavioral therapy is the most successful form of therapy for Prader-Willi syndrome patients. Generally, it doesn't seem like these people respond well to drugs.

❖ Syndrome of Landau-Kleffner

Aphasia (loss of language) is a symptom of unusual epilepsy known as Landau-Kleffner Syndrome, which typically appears between the ages of 3 and 7. It is frequently diagnosed in conjunction with autism and is twice as common in males than in females. These people initially experience normal, problem-free growth with typical speech and vocabulary. These people first lose their capacity for comprehension (also known as receptive speech), then their capacity for speaking (i.e., expressive speech). These modifications may happen gradually or abruptly.

When they are sleeping, people with Landau-Kleffner syndrome show aberrant EEG patterns (brain waves) in the occipital lobe and the temporoparietal-occipital areas of the brain. The typical method for diagnosing this syndrome is to look at the patient's EEG patterns while sleeping. 70% of people born with epilepsy eventually experience seizures that may or may not include convulsions.

Failure to react to sounds is one of Landau-Kleffner Syndrome's prevalent traits. As a result, parents may worry that their child has hearing issues. People with Landau-Kleffner Syndrome frequently exhibit autistic traits such as aggressiveness, poor eye contact, fixation on sameness, and sleep issues.

Unknown factors may contribute to Landau-Kleffner syndrome. Some hypothesized causes include a weakened immune system, viral exposure, and brain injury. The prognosis is better when speech therapy is initiated earlier, and the onset occurs after age 6. Corticosteroids and anticonvulsant medications, among others, have been proven to be helpful for many of these patients. The aberrant electrical brain activity pathways can be cut using a surgical procedure.

❖ **Fragile X**

A sex-related genetic condition called fragile X syndrome (sometimes called Martin-Bell syndrome) exists. Fragile X syndrome affects around 1.4 in 10,000 males and 0.9 in 10,000 girls. The exact frequency of this illness is unknown. Typically, males with this disease have a moderate to severe intellectual disability. Although they typically have a minor impairment, females can also be impacted.

15% to 20% of people with fragile X syndrome engage in behaviors similar to autism, such as poor eye contact, strange hand gestures, hand biting, and impaired sensory processing. Fragile X Syndrome is also frequently characterized by behavioral issues and speech-language delays.

A high-arched mouth, strabismus (lazy eye), huge ears, a long face, large testicles in men, weak muscular tone, flat feet, and occasionally moderate heart valve anomalies are further physical characteristics of those with fragile X syndrome. Some people with Fragile X syndrome do not have the conventional traits, even though most do (long face, huge ears).

Numerous medical facilities and labs use blood tests to identify Fragile X syndrome. Several therapies are advised for those with this illness, such as speech and language therapy, moderate medication for behavior issues, and sensory enhancement therapies. Families are urged to seek genetic counseling to learn about the inheritability of Fragile X Syndrome and to talk with family members about the possibility that other family members or future children may be affected.

❖ Williams Syndrome

A fragment of the DNA on chromosome 7 is missing in Williams Syndrome, sometimes referred to as Williams-Beuren syndrome, a rare genetic condition. One in 10,000 people have the condition or the prevalence rate.

Williams Syndrome is frequently associated with autistic symptoms. Some examples of these include delays in growth and language, issues with gross motor abilities, sensitivity to sounds, picky eating, and perseverance.

However, other symptoms of Williams Syndrome can call for alternative or additional therapy. To ensure the highest level of service, a diagnosis is necessary.

These people differ from the average autistic person in that they are sociable and have cardiovascular issues, high blood pressure, and excessive calcium levels. Additionally, they have distinct facial characteristics resembling fairies, such as almond-shaped eyes, oval ears, large lips, small chins, narrow faces, and wide mouths.

6.2 Activities and Exercises to Improve Mental Health

Coping Tool Box

1. Identify 1-5 Triggers

2. Identify 1-5 Warning Signs

3. Identify 1-5 Coping Techniques

4. Identify 1-5 strengths about yourself.

Daily Self-Reflection

1. What is one thing you are most grateful for today?

2. What was your biggest highlight from today?

3. What was one challenge you experienced today?

4. What is at least one thing you learned from that challenge?

5. What is one goal you plan to accomplish tomorrow?

Act of Kindness

Identify, list and do some acts of kindness and give yourself score.

Acts of Kindness Challenge

	Acts of Kindness	Kindness Score	Happiness Score	Completed
1	_____	_____	_____	☐
2	_____	_____	_____	☐
3	_____	_____	_____	☐
4	_____	_____	_____	☐
5	_____	_____	_____	☐
6	_____	_____	_____	☐
7	_____	_____	_____	☐
8	_____	_____	_____	☐
9	_____	_____	_____	☐
10	_____	_____	_____	☐
TOTAL SCORES		_____	_____	☐

My Stressors

Write your stressors which disturb your thoughts.

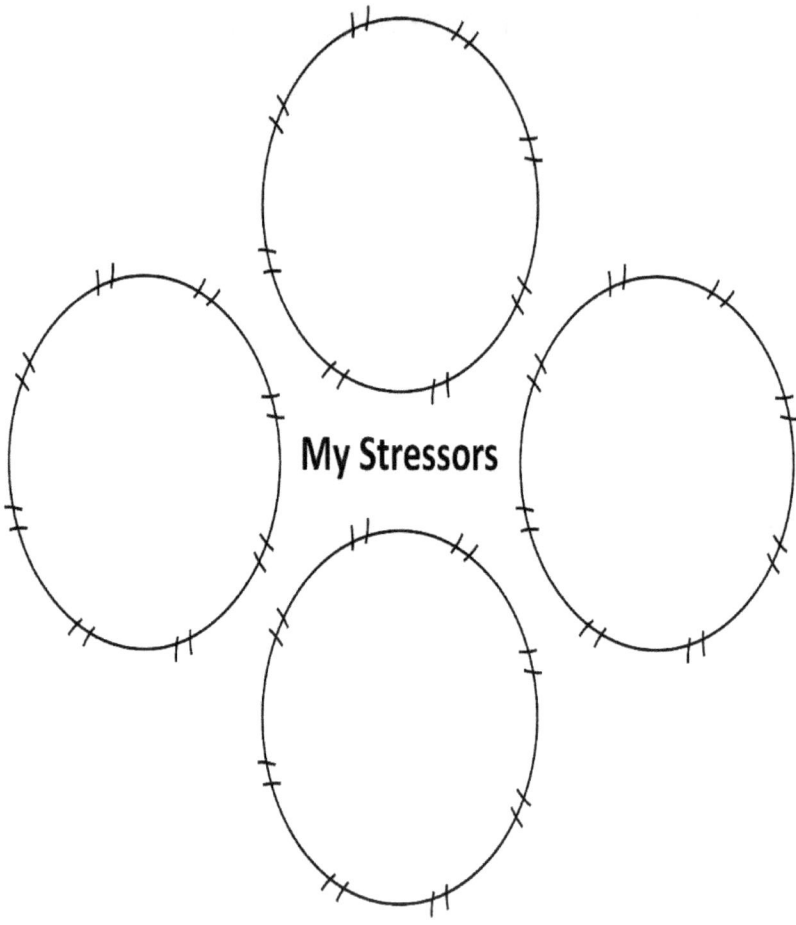

My Stressors

6.3 Mindfulness Techniques

It's easy to practice mindfulness. It is the capacity to know what is occurring and understand how it affects your feelings. It involves being in the present. The amygdala, the emotional area of the brain responsible for fear and stress reactions, is known to become less active when mindfulness practices are used.

What we do with our attention greatly impacts our mental health and happiness. Stress can make it difficult for us to be present, aware, and able to concentrate on making wise decisions. The practice of mindfulness resets the focus and creates room for wise choices, which improves overall well-being.

❖ **Advantages of Mindfulness**

For people of various ages, mindfulness has many advantages. According to research in the field of neuroscience, mindfulness enhances both brain health and general welfare. In particular, it can support the following:

- Our capacity to bring our attention back to the things around us, an activity or a task is strengthened through attention.
- *Emotional control*: Understanding our emotions enables us to understand when and why they occur. It's critical to acknowledge them, experience them completely, and then decide how to react to them.
- Understanding what other people are going through is made possible through compassion, which is the awareness of our thoughts and feelings.
- *Calming:* Mindful techniques, such as breathing exercises, aid in reducing tension in the body and mind.

Here are some easy mindfulness techniques you can teach your kid.

Glowing Jar: A clear jar should be filled with water, glitter, glycerin, or baby oil. This activity might work equally well with a snow globe. Ask your youngster to shake the jar and see the glitter settle after swirling, especially if they are experiencing a stressful day. This technique makes a potent metaphor connecting the inner condition of the mind to a visual object possible.

Observant Walks: Spend time walking through your neighborhood quietly while instructing your youngster to pay attention to every sound they notice. After that, ask them to summarize what they heard. They can be led to experience other feelings as well, such as the wind in their hair or the crunching of the leaves underfoot. You can ask an energetic child to run or skip so you can watch their heart rate or breathing rate change.

Researchers created the *Soles of the Feet* method to control angst, anger, and aggressiveness. You can teach your child to focus their awareness on a neutral body area, like the bottoms of their feet, while in emotionally charged situations. This method aids in calming and clearing the mind in tense and upsetting circumstances.

Ask your youngster to close their eyes and get comfortable while *focusing on breathing*. Pay attention to how it feels to breathe in and out. Ask them to place their hands on their stomachs to feel each breath's rise and fall. After roughly five cycles, you can direct them to any current emotions or thoughts. Tell them to watch those feelings and thoughts, then let them float away like a balloon. You are free to do this as many times as necessary or practical.

Ask your child to lie in bed, close their eyes, and _focus on different body regions_ while they drift off to sleep. Beginning at the toes, work your way carefully up to the head. This is a relaxing technique to help one feel grateful for their body by returning to it at the end of the day.

Exercise for Bell Listening: Ask your child to close their eyes and listen to the vibration of the bell as you ring a bell, whether it be a real bell, one from an app, or one that is online. After the ringing stops, instruct them to raise their hand and spend the next minute listening for any additional sounds. This straightforward but effective practice directs one's focus to the here and now and their surroundings.

A cooking game with a visual recipe. A fantastic hobby to promote awareness is cooking. Encourage your young learner to concentrate on their current job by having them prepare the ingredients, add them one at a time, and mix them in the proper order before seeing the combination bake or cook. Activities involving cooking also include a nice sensory element.

Meditation on raisins. For this children's mindfulness activity, give your child or each of your classmates a raisin. Use all five senses to practice examining and interacting with them. Utilize mindfulness to lessen anxiety, expand awareness, and experience more of life's simple pleasures.

Story stones for emotions. Children may learn about emotions by using charming build-a-face tale stones. Use them to instruct your kids or students to pay attention to their sentiments at the time. Another option is to discuss ways to relax when your emotions start to spiral out of control.

PLAY classical music. Children on the autistic spectrum can settle down with classical music. Your child will benefit from it as they learn to refocus and return to the present. You might play classical music in the background or give your kids or students earphones.

Sensory box use. Sensory boxes can be extremely useful for children on the autistic spectrum. They are a great addition to any mindfulness program because they are simple to produce and frequently enjoyed by autistic students. Use them to satisfy your child's sensory needs, bring back your child's attention to the present, and enhance learning and pleasure at home or school.

Use sensory toys to play. Numerous opportunities for mindfulness are presented by sensory play. Additionally, it makes people move more. To boost joy, balance the sensory system, reduce stress, and increase happiness, encourage your child or pupils to spend a set amount of time each day engaging in sensory activities.

Take a nature walk. Bring your little child on a nature stroll! In nature, there are countless opportunities to practice mindfulness. While you are out exploring, ask your child or children to listen to the sounds of the animals, water, and wind, seek for specific objects like leaves, pebbles, and insects, or even work on their field trip journals.

The Take-Home Message

Identifying your kid with autism's challenges and working with family, teachers, and wider support network, including doctors and therapists, are the keys to helping them improve. They must remember that they are not alone and that asking for aid is frequently the most crucial action. Another important thing to remember is that they shouldn't quit or become depressed over their problems. If they can persevere and keep trying, they are actively taking charge of their education, which can only result in gains.

Patients with ASD may benefit from medication, psychotherapy, cognitive therapy, occupational therapists, physiotherapy, and family treatments, among other treatments. These kids require individualized, multimodal evaluation and care. The design of therapies that enhance overall functioning must consider co-occurring disorders.

Although anxiety, depression and other disorders in ASD can be addressed separately as a diagnosis and should never be ignored, therapy should be modified for these people. Programs for infants with ASD or at risk for the disorder that focuses on teaching coping and resiliency skills may prevent symptoms from worsening.

You must interact with and nurture an autistic child's unique interests if you are an educator. Knowing more about your student's interests and preferences can help you better understand what drives them. Many people with autism have great artistic, mathematical, or physical passions. This may enable you to design classes that are more suitable for them and more effective, as well as to improve the atmosphere in which they learn. Teachers and parents can use various techniques discussed in the book to help autistic youngsters learn more effectively.

www.ingramcontent.com/pod-product-compliance
Lightning Source LLC
Chambersburg PA
CBHW070932120626
46546CB00004B/1392